Let's go by Bus

Barbara Hunter

Heinemann
LIBRARY

Little Nippers

H **www.heinemann.co.uk/library**
Visit our website to find out more information about **Heinemann Library** books.

To order:
☎ Phone 44 (0) 1865 888066
▤ Send a fax to 44 (0) 1865 314091
▢ Visit the Heinemann Bookshop at www.heinemann.co.uk/library to browse our catalogue and order online.

First published in Great Britain by Heinemann Library, Halley Court, Jordan Hill, Oxford OX2 8EJ, part of Harcourt Education.
Heinemann is a registered trademark of Harcourt Education Ltd.

Editorial: Jilly Attwood and Claire Throp
Design: Jo Hinton-Malivoire and bigtop, Bicester, UK
Models made by: Jo Brooker
Picture Research: Lodestone Publishing Limited
Production: Lorraine Warner

Originated by Dot Gradations
Printed and bound in China by South China Printing Company

10 digit ISBN 0 431 16461 4 (hardback)
13 digit ISBN 978 0 431 16461 8 (hardback)
06 05 04 03 02
10 9 8 7 6 5 4 3 2 1

10 digit ISBN 0 431 16466 5 (paperback)
13 digit ISBN 978 0 431 16466 3 (paperback)
07
10 9 8 7 6 5 4

British Library Cataloguing in Publication Data
Hunter, Barbara
Let's go by bus
388.3'22
A full catalogue record for this book is available from the British Library.

Acknowledgements
The publishers would like to thank the following for permission to reproduce photographs:
Alvey and Towers p. **4-5**, **7a**, **19**; Bubbles p. **13** (Loisjoy Thurstun); Eye Ubiquitous p. **7b** (Jason Burke), p. **12** (Davey Bold), p. **6a** (Paul Sehealt); James Davis Worldwide p. **6b**; Peter Evans p. **8-9**; Sally & Richard Greenhill Photo Library pp. **11**, **16-17** (Sally Greenhill); Sylvia Cordaiy Photo Library p. **20** (Milliken); Tografox pp. **10**, **14**, **15**, **18**, **21** (R. D. Battersby).

Cover photograph reproduced with permission of James Davis Travel Photography.

The publishers would like to thank Annie Davy for her assistance in the preparation of this book.

Every effort has been made to contact copyright holders of any material reproduced in this book. Any omissions will be rectified in subsequent printings if notice is given to the publishers.

Contents

Journeys

Have you ever been on a bus journey?

4

Many people go by bus. They are called passengers.

Why do people go by bus?

School

Shopping

Work

Holiday

On the road

Buses travel on the road.

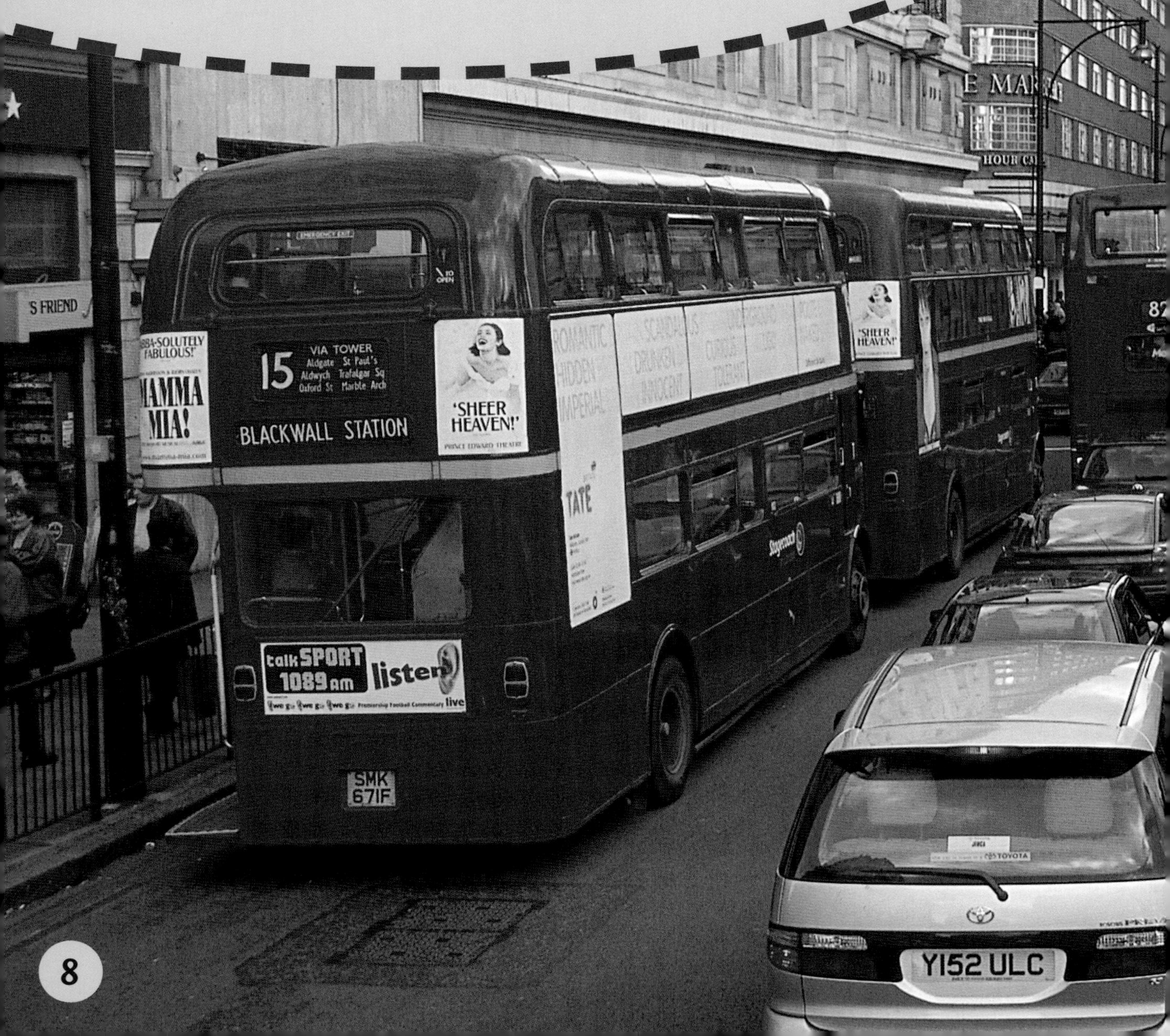

What else travels
on the road?

Timetable

Sometimes you need to look at a timetable to find out when the next bus will arrive.

Tunbridge Wells — Crowborough

Mondays to Fridays

	Bus No:	729	228	228	729	See Note 1 228	729	228	229
									0908
						0727	—	—	0921
						0738	—	—	0941
Willow Lea						0746 0802 0902			0942
Tonbridge, Castle, Stop E		0646	0649	0709	0747	0803 0903	0919	0942	
Tunbridge Wells, Meadow Road, Stop J		0647	0650	0710	0749	0805 0905	0921	0944	
Tunbridge Wells, War Memorial, Stop K		0649	0652	0712	0752	0808 0908	0924	0954	
Tunbridge Wells, opp. Rail Station, Stop T		0652	—	0715		0812	—	0928	0958
Old West Station, Sainsbury's							0917 0935	1005	
Showfields, Cherry Tree Road		0701	0701	0724	0801	0819 0919		0943	1013
Eridge Green, Church		0703	0703	0726	0803	0821 0925		0944	1014
Eridge Rail Station, By-Pass	arr.	0709	0709	0732	0809	0827		—	1017
	dep.	0709	0710	0733	0809	0827		—	1020
Crowborough Cross						0812	—		1024
South View Corner		0712	—		0815		—		
Whitehill, opp. Rose Court		0715						0947	
Alderbrook Estate		—	0713	0736		0830		0951	1030
Sir Henry Fermor School		—	0717	0740		0900		0957	—
Jarvis Brook, Rail Station (**See Note 1**)		—	0723	0746		0906		1001	—
Alderbrook Estate		—	0727	0750		0910		1004	—
Whitehill, Rose Court		—	0730	0753		0913			1034
South View Corner		—	0733	0756		0916		1007	1037
White Hart Inn									
Crowborough Cross									
Crowborough Leisure Centre									

NOTES
1. The 0727 Bus 228 from Willow Lea arrives at Jarvis Brook Rail Station at 0834 and departs at 0900. Bus 228 stops **opposite** Jarvis Brook Rail Station. Bus 229 stops **outside** Jarvis Brook Rail Station.
2. On non-schooldays, the 1530 Bus 228 departs Tonbridge at 1535. All other times through to Crowborough and Jarvis Brook are as shown.

At the bus stop

You need to wait for buses
in a queue at a bus stop.

How do you get
the bus to stop?

Tickets

Passengers need to have their money ready to pay the driver.

ticket

ticket machine

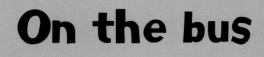

Passengers sit on seats on a bus. If it is busy some passengers have to stand up.

Stopping the bus

When you want to get off, you have to ring the bell.

Ding!

The bus stops at
the next stop.

Double-deckers

Some buses have an upstairs.

These are called double-deckers.

21

Shapes

What shapes can you see on a bus journey?

wheel

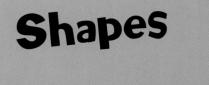

Index

The end

Notes for adults

This series supports the young child's knowledge and understanding of their world and, in particular, their mathematical development. Mathematical language like *heavy/light, long/short*, and an introduction to different shapes and positional vocabulary such as *near/far*, make this series useful in developing mathematical skills. The following Early Learning Goals are relevant to the series:
• find out about, and identify, some features of living things, objects and events that they observe
• show an awareness of similarities in shapes in the environment
• observe and use positional language.

The series explores journeys and shows four different ways of travelling and so provides opportunities to compare and contrast them. Some of the words that may be new to them in **Let's Go By Bus** are *passengers, timetable, arrive, queue* and *double-deckers*. Since words are used in context in the book this should enable the young child to gradually incorporate them into their own vocabulary.

The following additional information about bus journeys may be of interest:
There are many different types of bus including small inner city buses that take passengers on short distances and huge coaches that take passengers on long journeys. On some buses there are seat belts and foldaway seats to make space for wheelchairs and buggies. On some buses there is a driver and a conductor and sometimes an inspector who checks that all the passengers have a ticket.

Follow-up activities
The child could set up a road system using toys to re-enact or role play a special journey on a bus or coach. Alternatively, the child may enjoy making a record of their journey by drawing, writing or tape recording their experiences to share with others.